Ministers of Waxhaw Presbyterian Church

By S. David Carriker, D.Min.

ISBN 0-936013-71-0

Waxhaw Presbyterian Church
8100 Old Waxhaw-Monroe Road
Waxhaw, North Carolina

Preface to
Ministers of Waxhaw Presbyterian Church

Throughout the history of this church there have been 27 men and women who have been called 'Reverend,' 'Pastor' or 'Minister.' Some have held the role as a full-time Pastor, some as a Stated Supply and some as an Interim Supply. Even though the terms have changed recently, a stated supply is generally not full-time, yet supplies the church with regular preaching and other duties. An interim supply can be full or part-time, but has a focus on the transition or interim period between regular pastors.

There are also two individuals who have come from the ranks of the membership of the church to enter full-time ministry in the name of Jesus Christ. Of the 27 pastors, 26 were married and one was single, even though 2 more were single while in Waxhaw. Two pastors were divorced while in Waxhaw, one was married at Waxhaw and one died while serving as pastor in Waxhaw. The 26 married pastors had 52 children prior to arriving in Waxhaw, 5 while at the church and 8 after they left Waxhaw [for a total of 65 children]. But out of those who did have children, only one went into the ministry to serve God, Katherine Morton.

Many thanks to all of those who have helped with this project which began June 1, 2015 and ended June 12, 2016. I do hope you enjoy the work and give thanks to God for his blessings on this church.

---S. David Carriker, D.Min., Waxhaw, NC, July 4, 2016

Introduction

There are several lists in this work, in addition to individual brief biographies on each pastor. The master list gives basic information of birth, death, service dates and length of ministry. The individual biography contains information on the churches that were served by each of them.

The format of each biography is to give birth information, ancestry and situation, educational opportunities, occupational and ministerial services and finally, retirement and death information.

If at all possible a portrait is submitted and when none is available, a photograph of a highlight in their family is given.

Please feel free to contact me for any questions, concerns, corrections or notes that might be pertinent to a reprinting in the future.

---S. David Carriker

Table of Contents

Table of Contents
[continued]

The Ministers of

Waxhaw Presbyterian Church

The Ministers of Waxhaw Presbyterian Church- #1

During the summer months of 2015, I will feature one of our pastors as a bulletin insert each week. At the conclusion, you will receive the collection of the men and women of the church's history.

The first pastor at Waxhaw was the **Rev. Charles Wilson Harris Robinson**, who was named after Charles Wilson Harris, the first president of the University of North Carolina.

Charles W. Robinson, Class of 1879 at Columbia Seminary

He was born June 25, 1848 in Mississippi, the son of Col. Thomas Henderson Robinson and Catherine Hope Crawford.

It is not known where he attended school, but he finished Columbia Theological Seminary in 1879 and was ordained as a minister October 24, 1879, soon after this graduation photo was taken in June.

He married Ellen Lavinia Rogers 10/21/1880 and they had three children: Olivia [1881], Edmund [1885] and Ellen [1889, while in Waxhaw]. His wife, Ellen, died in 1906, at the age of 48.

He helped form this church in its infancy and preached here from the organization on October 19, 1888 until August 31, 1890. Here is a memorial to his life and service to God:

3

In the 1894 *Minutes of the General Assembly,* Winston Second Church is listed, with C. W. Robinson, pastor, one Elder, one Deacon, 13 Added on Examination, 10 Added on Certificate; Total Communicants — 23. C. W. Robinson, the pastor listed in the two statements above, was the Reverend Charles W. H. Robinson, who was received from the Presbytery of Mecklenburg in 1893 and who remained a member of the Presbytery of Orange until his church was placed in the Presbytery of Winston-Salem upon its erection in 1923. Mr. Robinson was a native of Mississippi, a graduate of Davidson College (Class of 1874) and Columbia Seminary (Class of 1879), and was licensed by the Presbytery of Concord, April 12, 1878. Prior to his work in what was to be the Presbytery of Winston-Salem, Mr. Robinson was ordained by the Presbytery of Louisville (Ky.), October 24, 1879, in which he served as pastor of the Glasgow church. In 1884 he returned to North Carolina where he was pastor of the Sugar Creek, Monroe, Graham Street (Charlotte), and Gastonia churches. Except for a very brief period, during which he was at the Elkin and Worthville churches, he served the North Wilkesboro Church from 1895 until his retirement, caused by ill health, in 1936. Mr. Robinson died in North Wilkesboro on January 11, 1938.

The Rev. C. W. Robinson

4

Under his ministry, the people of the church banded together and built the first sanctuary on land donated by the railroad company in 1890. The early church building stood high on the bluff overlooking the railroad and the town of Waxhaw, as the highest point around.

The first wooden sanctuary [1890-1929] which stood on the same foundation as the second brick sanctuary.

We give thanks to God for his ministry and faith.

Pastors of Waxhaw Presbyterian Church- #2

John Logan McLees was the 2nd pastor of Waxhaw Presbyterian Church, arriving as a "Supply Pastor" along with Rev. Robinson, the 1st pastor in 1888. Rev. Robinson was 40 years old and Rev. McLees was 44.

These two men shared in the responsibilities for the newly developed church in Waxhaw on land that was given to the church [a full-square city block] by the Georgia, Carolina & Northern Railway, a subsidiary of Seaboard Air Line Company.

He was born May 25, 1844 in Greenwood, SC to Rev. John McLees [1812-1882] and Sarah Cornelia Anderson. John's younger brother, Richard Gustavus McLees [1864-1956] was also a Presbyterian minister. He grew up on the family farm and was himself a farmer by occupation.

John Logan McLees
Columbia Theological
Seminary, Class of 1885

He attended Adger College in Walhalla, SC and received a BA in 1879. The school no longer exists, but began in 1877 and closed in 1887. It was on the site of the later Newberry College. He taught school in Brunswick, GA from 1879-1881, when he entered Columbia Theological Seminary. He graduated in 1885 and was licensed to preach by the South Carolina Presbytery April 15, 1885.

He was then ordained in Mecklenburg Presbytery October 30, 1885 in order to preach at Providence PC on Providence Road. He remained there until early 1888 and moved to the Graham Street PC in Charlotte and the assistant pastor at 2nd PC in Charlotte. Both merged and became what we know as the Covenant PC today. He labored at these two churches and preached in Waxhaw 1888-1889 before moving to Orangeburg PC in Orangeburg, SC [1889-1925].

In Orangeburg, he met and married Annie Leah Cornelson [1873-1946] about 1891. They had the following children: Angie [1892], Cornelia [1895], George [1897], John L., Jr. [1899] and Arthur [1908].

He died there April 21, 1925 after serving that church for 36 years and serving God for almost 40 years.

May we thank God for His providence in sending **John Logan McLees** to Waxhaw!

The Ministers of Waxhaw Presbyterian Church #3

Henderson Makemie Dixon was born in the Steele Creek community of Mecklenburg Co., NC on September 18, 1860, to Hugh Mack Dixon and Margaret Hoey [Howie].

He studied at Davidson College and UNC before entering Princeton Theological Seminary in 1885. He graduated in 1888 and was licensed in Mecklenburg Presbytery after graduation.

Later in the same year he was ordained as an evangelist for Charleston Presbytery, serving there from 1888-1891. While he was there, he met and married Carrie Victoria Hammond on Beech Island, SC in 1890.

On March 1, 1891 he accepted a call as pastor of Monroe First PC and supplied Waxhaw PC for the same period. He was the first pastor to enjoy the new church building built in 1890. He then moved to McColl, SC from 1902-1905.

He became a professor at Flora McDonald College and also served the Philadelphius PC nearby from 1905-1924, when ill health caused him to resign from active ministry.

REV. H. M. DIXON, B. D.

DEDICATION

In token of our deep love and appreciation for his years of service to us, we, the Class of Nineteen Twenty-four, dedicate to

Rev. H. M. Dixon

This fourth volume of The White Heather

From the 1938 annual [The White Heather] College in Red Springs, NC

Henderson was named after the first Presbyterian minister to America, Rev. Francis Makemie.

He and his wife had one daughter, Catherine [b. 1892] while they served Waxhaw.   He resided in Augusta, GA 1925-1937 and died at Beech Island, SC on September 5, 1937.

We thank God for his 50 years of service to the Kingdom of God.

The Ministers of Waxhaw Presbyterian Church- #4

The Reverend **William Kennedy Boggs** was the fourth pastor [supply] of Waxhaw Presbyterian church from October 1, 1895 until his death on October 16, 1896 at the age of 46, less two days.

He was born October 18, 1850 in Liberty, SC to George William Barzili and Elizabeth K. McWhorter and attended Carmel PC. He had three other Boggs cousins who were ministers also.

W.K. Boggs was a farmer prior to his entering Columbia Theological Seminary in 1882 at age 32. He graduated in 1885, but was not licensed until 1888 in the South Carolina Presbytery, where he began ministry as a stated supply in the Central PC in Anderson, SC [1888-89]. He then went on as a stated supply at the Bethiah PC and Willington PC in the Abbeville, SC area [1890-91]. Both churches folded a century ago.

He was then ordained in Augusta Presbytery in 1891 and pastored the Sibley PC near Augusta, GA [1891-93] {closed}. From there he was an evangelist in Blackstock, SC [1893-95] and pastor at Waxhaw PC [1895-1896].

His obituary states he died at home in Waxhaw on October 16, 1896 of fever and 'erysipelas.' This is an old term [lit.: red skin] for a severe skin rash, usually on any of the legs, arms and face. It is a strep bacteria of the upper dermis. He is buried in the Westview Cemetery in Liberty, SC.

Boggs was only in ministry for 8 years, but left a wife and six children to survive him: Mary Elizabeth [Alexander] Boggs {married 2/23/1872}, and Eliza Estelle [b. 1873], Sarah Etta [b.1876], Mary Inez [b. 1877], Nina Gertrude [1879], Leland [b. 1882], Josephine [b.1884], Willie [b. 1888] and Paul [b.1892].

Rev. William Black in 1896 stated "during his brief sojourn in this presbytery he supplied as pastor the church at Waxhaw for part of his time, spending the remainder in evangelistic work. He had peculiar gifts, fitting him for evangelistic work and was greatly blessed in his labors, preaching the gospel with ranch power and fearlessly, yet kindly,

Tombstone for Rev. W.K. Boggs denouncing sin in every form. Wherever he labored special emphasis was laid upon the privilege and duty of family prayer and many are the family altars erected through his influence."

There is one marital record that he performed: Maggie Broom, 17, to James P. Garrison, 24, on October 16, 1895 [at a home].

Bethiah Presby. Church, closed- Boggs pastored here

Carmel Presby. Church, 1787- Boggs was raised here

**Willington Presbyterian Church, memorialized-
Boggs pastored here**

Every church that Rev. Boggs pastored has closed!

May we give thanks to God for his service in the Kingdom.

The Ministers of Waxhaw Presbyterian Church- #5

The 5th minister in Waxhaw was **Hugh William Hoon**. He was born 5/27/1872 in Mercer, PA as the son of Robert & Sarah Hoon. He was a student at Mari College and then studied theology under Erie Presbytery [PA] and then Mecklenburg Presbytery [NC].

The Waxhaw Institute
(The Waxhaw Normal and Collegiate Institute)

He was the principal of the Forest City Normal College [1894-1896]. He was then licensed to preached 5/14/1896 and ordained 4/22/1897 by Mecklenburg Presbytery. He was the pastor of Waxhaw PC and founder & president of the newly formed Waxhaw Normal and Collegiate Institute from 1897-1900. The school continued until prior to 1910 when the state reported that they failed to submit and annual report.

From Waxhaw he became the assistant pastor of Second PC in Charlotte on N. Tryon St. and pastor of East Side Chapel [now, Caldwell Memorial PC] from 1901-1903.

In 1904 he moved to Utica PC in San Antonio, Texas where he met and married Adele Phillips. They had two daughters, Manira [1905] and Carolyn [1915]. From there he moved to 1st Stamford, TX 1909-1910 [UPCUS], which became 1st Taylor, TX 1910-1916 [PCUS]. He was also the moving spirit in organizing Westminster Encampment, Kerrville, TX. It was like a Texas form of Montreat, without the mountains! It continued until 1950.

Hoon died of pneumonia 3/4/1916 at age 45. He left behind a young wife of 30, and a 14 year old daughter and 1 year old daughter. He is

15

memorialized at Schreiner College, where a dormitory is named after him in Kerrville, TX in 1926.

Hoon Building
Schreiner College

Let us give thanks to God for the ministry of Rev. Hoon, who served God in Waxhaw [his first church] and five other churches, as principal of two colleges and as the organizer of a church retreat and camp. Praise God!

Tombstone [left]

HUGH W. HOON
MAY 27 1871
MAR. 4 1916

Church Memorial [below]

**Taylor Presbyterian Church, Kerrville, TX,
built under the ministry of Rev. Hugh W. Hoon**

The Ministers of Waxhaw Presbyterian Church- #6

John Howie Dixon was the 6th minister to serve Waxhaw PC. He was the brother of our 3rd pastor, Henderson Dixon. John Dixon was born 9/1/1852 to Hugh Mack Dixon & Margaret Howie in the Steele Creek Community of Mecklenburg Co., NC. He grew up as a farmer with the family. He graduated from UNC and then began teaching. He graduated from Union Theological Seminary in Richmond, VA 1877-1880 and was licensed to preach 4/16/1881 by Mecklenburg Presbytery, PCUS.

With that he began to teach in Rutherfordton, NC while he was a stated supply at the church there 1881-82. He then crossed the South Carolina line and was the stated supply in Gaffney 1882-83. From there he went to Munfordville, KY as stated supply 1883-85 and was ordained into the ministry by Louisville Presbytery 12/4/1884.

From Kentucky he moved to Carrollton, MO as a stated supply 1885-86. His 5th pastorate was in Gainesville, GA as stated supply 1886-88, followed by Sparta, GA in 1888. He then moved to Florence, SC for his first full-time pastorate [1888-98]. He married Loula Erwin [1869-1925] in 1896 in Mecklenburg Co., NC before moving to Sharon PC (SC) and Blacksburg PC [1898-1901].

That is when he moved to Waxhaw for his 10th pastorate, while also serving at Matthews PC 1901-06. From here he moved on as stated supply in Winder, GA [and group] in 1906 and then came back to the Tar Heel State to Laurel Hill, Aberdeen & Smyrna churches 1907-1917 as pastor, with this interesting story:

A happy event of interest occurred near Johns Station last Wednesday afternoon, March 17, 1909, at the home of Mr. and Mrs. J. W. Jernigan, when their charming daughter, Miss Katie, became the bride of Mr. Kenneth Watson, of Hamlet. Only a few relatives and friends of the contracting parties witnessed the happy event. The parlor was tastefully decorated with ivy for the occasion. The Wedding March was sweetly rendered by Mrs. J. H. Dixon, and at the first soft tones the bride entered, leaning on the arm of the groom, dressed in bewitching white messaline, carrying a beautiful bouquet of lilies of the valley and ferns. Rev. J. H. Dixon, in his impressive manner, spoke the solemn words that made them man and wife. After the soleum vows had been taken, and congratulations of relatives and friends had been received, Mr. and Mrs. Watson boarded the 7 o'clock train at John's, amid showers of rice, for Jacksonville, St. Agustine and other Southern pointe. Besides best wishes, they received several beautiful and useful presents. They will make their home in Hamlet, N. C., were the groom is employed as conductor on the Seaboard line from Hamlet to Wilmington. Their many friends wish them much happiness all through life.

He then moved to Charlotte as pastor of Pegram St. PC [now, Plaza] from 1917-19.

He died there 1/12/1919 and is buried in Charlotte at the Mallard Creek Cemetery.

Let us give thanks for the ministry and life of John Dixon.

The Ministers of Waxhaw Presbyterian Church- #7

The seventh minister of the church was **John Logan McKinstry**

John Logan McKinstry

[from 11/1/1906 to 10/31/1908]. He was born 7/17/1878 in Macon, TN to John Wilson McKinstry and Pinkie Eldorado Parrott. Rev. McKinstry was raised on the family farm, where he worked, until he enrolled in South Western Presbyterian University [TN, 1899-1903]. After graduating with a BA, he continued with their divinity school [1903-06] and graduated with a BD. He was licensed to preach by Memphis Presbytery in 1908 and ordained to preach 10/19/1908 by Mecklenburg Presbytery. While in Waxhaw he was paired with the Siler PC to preach the gospel.

He married Margaret Gordon Rothrock in 1908 as well. From here he went as Stated Supply to Hugo PC in Hugo, OK [1909-11]. He then went as pastor to Clarksville, TN [1911-14]. From there he continued in ministry as the pastor of Magnolia PC in Magnolia, MS [1914-16]. They had five children: Margaret [1909], Mary Ann [1912], John R. [1914], Martha [1921] and Nancy [1927].

After this he is listed doing 'secular work' in Warren, TN [1916-20]. He then was a Stated Supply at the Neshobo, TN group of churches [1921-22]. He then was a teacher in the following Tennessee schools: Grand Junction [1923], Saulsbury [1924], Harriman [1925], Saltillo [1926-28], and finally, Reagan school [1928-32].

Rev. McKinstry then became the Stated Supply at the Germantown PC, TN [1932-34] before being without charge in Reagan, TN [1934-37] where he returned to farming. At age 60 he moved to the Blue Mountain, MS in 1938 and returned to teaching there in 1941.

He died February 15, 1955 [age 76½] from stomach cancer and is buried next to his wife in the Sardis Cemetery, Memphis, TN.

We give thanks to God for the 49-year ministry of teaching and preaching of Rev. John McKinstry and the labor that he gave during his two year stay in Waxhaw and Wesley Chapel.

The Ministers of Waxhaw Presbyterian Church- #8

{the Philadelphus PC (still stands) will **Rev. Pace** in the vestibule}

George Thomas Pace was the 8th minister to serve at Waxhaw PC. He was born 10/20/1865 in Clarksville, TN, the son of William P. Pace & Annie Jane Harris. He was raised on the family farm and then went to school at South West Presbyterian University [1888-1896] and Union Theological Seminary [1896-99].

He was licensed to preach 9/14/1899 and ordained in 1900 by Fayetteville Presbytery. He began as supply of the Barbecue PC [1899-1900] and then taught at the McCallum School [1900-03] in Philadelphus, NC and nearby Flora McDonald College [1903-07]. He served Parkton PC in Parkton [1901-03], Dundarrach PC and the Westminster School.

While in the Red Springs area he met and married Katherine Isabelle Brown 8/26/1907 in the Philadelphus PC. They had one daughter,

23

Katherine Isabelle Pace [7/27/1908-9/30/1908]. At the college he taught all of the Natural Science courses from Health to Physics. Rev. Pace served as pastor for Waxhaw from Jan. 1 to Oct. 16 in 1910 but then returned to Robeson Co., NC

Rev. Pace died 6/1/1936 of an abscess of the spleen and malarial fever. He is buried next to his mother, wife and child at Philadelphus PC.

Let us give thanks to God for his ministry of 37 years, in Waxhaw, Red Springs and Barbecue churches.

The Ministers of Waxhaw Presbyterian Church- #9
The ninth minister at Waxhaw PC was **Charles Edward Robertson**.

Charles E. Robertson

He was born 2/16/1851 and came to Waxhaw 1/1/1911.
He was born in Montgomery, AL to John Harris Robertson and Susanah Morris Foster. He grew up on the family farm and began his education at Alabama Polytechnic Institute in 1875.

Upon graduation in 1878 he began to work. Robertson married Chloe Ligon in Alabama 8/10/1881 and they had two daughters, one of which died young.

Chloe died in 1899, leaving Rev. Robertson a widower. He had entered Columbia Theological Seminary in 1890 and graduated in 1894 and was then licensed 7/3/1893 and ordained 7/7/1894 in Enoree Presbytery.

He began ministry as pastor at the Limestone PC in Gaffney [1894-1901]. He then moved to Conway PC in SC [1901-1908], where he met and married Sue Rollinson 11/1901. He had three more daughters in this marriage.

After Conway he moved to Erick & Cheyenne PC in Mangum Presbytery, OK [1908-09] as a stated supply and then the Central PC in Lawton, OK as stated supply [1910].

He then moved to Waxhaw as the pastor of Waxhaw PC and Walkersville PC [1911-1918]. While here he led the church through

World War I, while experiencing the loss of Ney McNeely, I. Ney was appointed as the Consul of Aden, but on his first trip there was killed when a German U-boat, U-38, sunk the ship *Persia* off of Crete in late 1916. Ney McNeely, I was the uncle of Ney McNeely, II the one that we all knew.

The War ended right after Rev. Robertson left Waxhaw in July 1918. He went to Edisto Island, SC as pastor [1918-1929] and then retired in Walterboro, SC [1930-33].

When his second wife died in 1934, he moved back to Conway to be with her family. In 1940 he moved back to Walterboro and died there 8/8/1942.

REV. CHARLES EDWARD ROBERTSON
FEB. 16, 1851
AUG. 8, 1942
"A FAITHFUL SERVANT OF GOD"

Let us give thanks to God for the service of Charles Edward Robertson.

The Ministers of Waxhaw Presbyterian Church- #10

George Brazier Thompson was the 10th pastor of Waxhaw Presbyterian Church. He was born 1/29/1874 in New Orleans, LA to Edward Thomas Thompson & Amelia Ann Case. His father was a steamboat mate, but had been unemployed for 8 months in 1880. He ran a steam-boat from New Orleans to Florida, where he met his wife Amelia. Little George must have spent much time on the steamboat growing up.

He graduated from King College (TN) with a B.Ph. and continued to Union Theo. Sem. 1904-07 [B.Div.]. Thompson was ordained by the Durant Presbytery 10/6/1907 and began pastoring at Hugo 1st PC, OK 1907-08, then Oxford, NC 1908-1911.

There, he met and married Anita Christine Brown on 8/11/1909. They returned to Bristol, TN at the Windsor Ave. PC 1911-12, where he then became a professor at King College in Bible & Philosophy

1912-19. While the Thompsons were in Tennessee, their two children were born: Edward Arlington [1914] and Edna Jean [1918]. While there, Rev. Thompson was the Stated Clerk of Holston Presbytery.

The Thompsons came to Waxhaw in 1919 and remained in 1923. 36 new members were received during his tenure at the church, but there were 43 losses [11 deaths, 22 distant transfers and 10 area transfers.]

From Waxhaw, Rev. Thompson proceeded to Great Falls, SC [1923-26] before moving to Milledgeville, GA [1926-29]. He was without charge in Rossville, GA [1930-32] during the depression and then moved to New Providence PC in McAfee, KY [1933-42]. His final pastorates were in Millersburg PC and Shawhan PC [KY] [1942-44].

He died in Lexington, KY 3/18/1944 after being hospitalized for 24 days at the age of 70. His death was due to a pulmonary embolism after the removal of his gall bladder.

Let us give thanks to God for his service to our Lord and Savior!

The Ministers of Waxhaw Presbyterian Church- #11

Charles Eugene Kingsley was the 11th pastor of Waxhaw Presbyterian Church. He was born 5/20/1860 in eastern Tennessee in Jefferson County to Roswell Erasmus Kingsley and Nancy Josephine Worley. He grew up on the family farm, but eventually became a bee-keeper at the age of 20. A year later [10/2/1881] he married Alice M. Farnsworth in Tennessee and they began their new life together. Their children were Ethel [1882] and May [1886].

Mr. and Mrs. C. E. Kingsley, 1914-1921

It is possible that Charles Eugene Kingsley was named after the famous Rev. Charles Kingsley, the Chaplain of Queen Victoria in England.

He graduated from Tusculum College (Greenville, TN) and continued to Seminary. He was ordained by the St. Johns Presbytery in 1904 and began pastoring a group of churches in Palmetto, FL in 1907. He then moved on the Leesburg PC [Dade City, FL] and Parrish PC, FL 1908-11.

He then came to Pineville PC, NC from 1912-13 and then Providence PC and Matthews PC 1914-21.

The Kingsley's then moved to Rome, GA where he was a Presbytery evangelist in 1922. He was then without charge in 1923 in Lithia, FL before coming to Waxhaw from May 1, 1924-March 1, 1926.

During his 22-month stay in Waxhaw, the church gained 19 new members, but there were 21 losses [4 deaths, 3 distant transfers and 14 area transfers.]

From Waxhaw, Rev. Kingsley proceeded to Troy PC and Elm Corner PC [KY, 1926-28] before moving back to Lithia, FL [1928-30] as an evangelist there. His final churches were Mango PC and Gardenville PC in Florida 1930-33.

He died there 6/1/1933 and is buried in the Bloomingdale Community Cemetery.

Let us give thanks to God for his service to our Lord and Savior in Waxhaw, in other churches and in the Kingdom!

The Ministers of Waxhaw Presbyterian Church- #12

The Twelve minister at Waxhaw Presbyterian Church was **Thomas Franklin Grier** of Gaston Co., NC. He was the son of William Alexander Grier & Belle Crawford and was born 10/27/1885. The Griers [not related to Karen **Greer**] are generally from the Associate Reformed Presbyterian Church or a descendant of it.

It is uncertain is Thomas was the one who left that denomination, but he did attend Erskine College [1904-08] and Seminary [1909], both ARP schools, before moving on to Louisville Theological Seminary [1910 {PCUS}]. He is then listed with ill health, living on the farm. He was not licensed until 4/14/1926 or ordained until 1927 by Mecklenburg Presbytery.

Thomas Franklin Grier

Just prior to coming to Waxhaw, Thomas married Mary Knox Dickey 8/5/1925 in San Antonio, TX. Then the new couple came to Waxhaw PC (NC) [1925-28] and Six Mile Creek PC [1926-28 {in the new Faith PC location on US #521}]. While they were here, a daughter was born to Thomas & Mary, named Mary M. Grier [1926]. She evidently died before 1930.

He then was the pastor at Tirzah PC and Waxhaw PC (SC) in Bethel Presbytery, SC [1928-42]. From there Thomas Grier went to the Pleasant Grove PC, Catholic PC and Hebron PC [1942-56]. He was then a temporary supply [1956-60] before being honorably retired in 1960.

He died 6/16/1965. Both Thomas & Mary are buried at the Steele Creek PC Cemetery.

Steele Creek Presbyterian Church

Let us give thanks to God for his brief ministry with us in Waxhaw.

The Ministers of Waxhaw Presbyterian Church- #13

The 13th minister at Waxhaw Presbyterian Church was **Carleton**

Moravian College & Seminary

Emory White of Winston-Salem, NC. He was the son of James Emory White & Mary Lee Grubb and was born 7/24/1883. His father was a house carpenter and builder and by 17 Carleton worked at the tobacco plant in Winston-Salem.

About 1901 he entered the Moravian College in Winston-Salem and graduated 3 years later. He then enter the Moravian Theological Seminary and graduated in 1908. He was ordained by the Moravians on 3/28/1909 and served in two churches:
Mayodan Moravian Church [1909-1912] and
Greensboro Moravian Church [1912-1916].

In 1916 he transferred to the Presbyterian Church, US and served in it for 31 years. He began in Roxboro PC [1916-1919] and then Marshville PC [1919-1930] & Waxhaw PC [1928-1930], both while living in Marshville. It was Rev. White who was instrumental in having the old first-wooden sanctuary torn down [Ney McNeely said he helped as an 8 year old boy!] so that the new second-brick sanctuary could be built [1929-1998].

Second Brick sanctuary [1929-1998]

He married [8/25/1909] Erma Pearl Pfaff in Winston-Salem and they had five boys: Carlton Edward [1911], Lewis Rights [1913], Harold Eugene [1915], Bernard [1921] and Wilbur Agnew [1923]. They also had one daughter who died young: Marjorie Louise [1917-1919]. The family moved to Chase City, VA in 1930 and remained there for 8 years. He then served the Blue Ridge PC group of churches in Roan Presbytery {TN} [1938-1945] and then the Harmony PC & Roller PC in Sykesville, Maryland [1945-1947]. While he was in Virginia he was an avid supporter of the Hampden-Sydney College. In his

Presbytery obituary, a church member described him as "well-informed and a convincing preacher; a builder of churches and a sympathetic pastor."

He died there 1/21/1947 and is buried in the Springfield Cemetery, Sykesville, MD.

Let us give thanks to God for his faithful service.

The Ministers of Waxhaw Presbyterian Church- #14

The 14th minister at Waxhaw Presbyterian Church was **James Fraser Cocks** of Manchester, England. He was born 11/5/1871 to Samuel William Cocks and Margaret Bell. He married Rosa Helen Luesing 1905.

Manitoba College

After graduation from high school he enrolled as a student at Manitoba College [graduated 1898] in Winnipeg, Manitoba, Canada, after which he was accepted at the University of Manitoba and graduated four years later [1902] with a BA degree. He must have sensed a call from God and went back to the Manitoba College campus to attend their Theological Seminary. But within the year he transferred to Louisville Theological Seminary {PCUS} in Louisville, KY [1904-06].

He then went to Lane Theological Seminary [1908-09], a prominent Northern Presbyterian Seminary, famous for its anti-slavery emphasis in the 1830-1865 period. He then went to the Oskalooska

Lane Theological Seminary

College in Iowa [1913-17] where he received a Master's Degree and a PhD. He was licensed 4/1904 and ordained 5/11/1904 by the Louisville Presbytery of the UPCUSA.

He was the pastor of Alliance PC in Louisville [1904-06] and then became a teacher and stated supply in Prestonburg, KY [1907] before moving to Madisonville, KY [1908-09]. From there he ventured to Punta Gorda, FL [1910] before transferring to the PCUS as a stated supply in Sarasota, FL [1910-15].

After nine years in Florida, the call to Canada returned to his heart. He transferred to the Presbyterian Church of Canada as the secretary of Toronto Presbytery, while working as the chaplain at the YMCA camps and the YMCA hospital [1915-18]. He returned once again to America as the pastor of Bethany PC {UPCUSA} in Buffalo, NY [1919-21].

He then returned to the PC of Canada as pastor of the Chalmers PC in Hamilton, Ontario [1922-26]. He then came to the South again in the PCUS as the pastor of Inman Park in Atlanta, GA [1926-28], Summerville PC in SC [1928-30] and then the North Charlotte PC, along with Waxhaw PC [1931-33]. He was here during the depths of the Great Depression.

Nine people joined the church by their profession of faith in Christ, four died and 11 transferred to other churches. He then lived without a charge [church] in Charlotte for 1934-35. At the age of 65 he ventured to Florida again as the stated supply of Ft. Meade PC [1936-38] and then retired in 1940 in Sarasota.

He died there 8/30/1943 and is buried in Bradenton, FL in the Manasota Cemetery.

Let us thank God for his service during a difficult time here.

The Ministers of Waxhaw Presbyterian Church- #15

The 15th minister at Waxhaw Presbyterian Church was **Ewell Van Buren Wiley**. He was our first minister born in the 20th Century, on 6/13/1902, in Mill Point, WV to John Francis Wiley and Augusta Roberta Smith. John was a shoe maker and died when Van was young.

Van grew up in Marlinton, West Virginia and then attended Hampden-Sydney College [1922-26, BA] in Virginia and Union Theological Seminary [1927-30, BD]. After seminary he was licensed and ordained 7/15/1930 by Mangum Presbytery.

Ewell Van Buren Wiley

He went to his first churches in Oklahoma, Carnegie PC [pastor] & Gotebo PC [stated supply] in [1930-31]. While there he married Agnes Lee Dunlop 11/26/1931 of Gotebo, OK. After the wedding they went to Weatherford PC [1931-32].

He then came to Waxhaw PC and Providence PC in 1934 and remained for 13 years and 9 months. While he was here he led the congregation through the Great Depression, into recovery. He led the congregation into the beginning of World War II and through the end of the war. 138 members were added to the roll over those year [10/yr.] During the same 13¾ year period, 11 people died and 53 people transferred to other churches, giving a net increase of 74 new members. The only name in his list I recognize is the last one to join in 1948: Melvin Faris.

Rev. Wiley was the second longest serving minister here, after Rev. Morton [14 yr., 7 mo.]. Along with John Gerstenmier [10 yrs., 1 mo.], they are the only three ministers to serve over 10 years at Waxhaw PC. On 7/1/2016 I will become the 4th of 27 ministers to join this group of clergy. Attached is his installation bulletin for 10/21/1934.

When Rev. Wiley left Waxhaw he went to Norwood PC [NC, 1948-51] and then to the Concord PC & Loray PC in Iredell Co., NC [1951-56]. He had a heart attack at age 54 and died while in surgery 8/18/1956.

Let us thank God for his ministry in Waxhaw and the in the Kingdom of God.

Waxhaw Presbyterian Church

Waxhaw, North Carolina

Organized 1889   Erected 1930

Sunday Services

Sunday School - - - - -	10:00 A. M.
Young People - - - - -	6:30 P. M.
Preaching - - - -	11:00 A. M.-7:30 P. M.

Preaching Services—First, Third and Fifth Sundays

7:30 P. M., Sunday, October 21, 1934

INSTALLATION OF REV. E. V. WILEY BY A COMMISSION OF MECKLENBURG PRESBYTERY:

Rev. J. G. Garth, Presiding; Rev. D. P. McGeachy, Sermon; Rev. J. W. Stork, D.D., Charge the Pastor; Mr. L. M. Ennis, Charge the People; Mr. W. R. McDonald, Mr. W. E. Price.

43

The Ministers of Waxhaw Presbyterian Church- #16

The 16th minister at Waxhaw Presbyterian Church was **Jack Robert Tackett**. Rev. Tackett was born 6/22/1898, the last of our ministers to be born in the 19th Century! He was the son of Walter Purdue Tackett & Katherine Dyson of Lexington, MS.

Walter Tackett was a lawyer in Lexington and sent his son to South Western Presbyterian University [1916-18], the University of Mississippi [1918-19] and Union Theological Seminary [1922-25].

J. R. Jackett.

His father died in 1910 and he stayed home with his mother for her support. After graduation, Central Mississippi licensed & ordained him 10/1925.

From there he began his ministry as the pastor of the Ackerman PC in MS and the group of churches yoked with it [1925-36]. While he was there he met and married Susan Routh Clarke from Midway, KY 5/9/1933. They had one daughter, Evelyn Dulaney Tackett [1934-2012].

The Tacketts then moved to the Atoka group of churches in TN [1936-38] before moving back to Durant, MS as pastor [1938-41]. He then went to the Mt. Olive PC & Hopewell PC, MS [1941-46]. He proceeded into the Tar Heel State at Bethany PC & Altan PC as pastor [1947-48] and Waxhaw PC & Banks PC [1949-50].

Back to MS he went as pastor of the Newton PC, Mt. Moriah PC & Roberts PC in Newton, MS [1950-57] and then Ackerman, Bywy & Old Lebanon PC in MS [1957-65]. His final pastorate was at the Utica & Lebanon churches in Learned, MS [1965-67].

He retired 7/1/1968 and was later dismissed to the Mississippi Valley Presbytery 7/19/1973 of the Presbyterian Church of America.

He died in Jackson, MS 1/15/1984. All three of the Tacketts are buried at the Odd Fellows Cemetery in Lexington, Mississippi.

Let us give thanks to God for his service in the church.

The Ministers of Waxhaw Presbyterian Church- #17

The 17th minister to serve Waxhaw Presbyterian Church was **Charles Wayne Potter**. He was born 2/5/1918 in Hansonville, MD, the son of John Michael Potter and Edith Williams.

He studied at Emory University in Atlanta, GA [1935-36], Presbyterian College in Clinton, SC [1936-38] and Wheaton College in Wheaton, IL [1938-39] with a Bachelor of Arts degree. From there he returned to Atlanta to Columbia Theological Seminary [1939-43] with a Bachelor of Div. degree.

While he was in seminary, he met and married Agnes Tinsley Wharton of Long Beach, MS on 9/5/1941. They had no children.

He was licensed and ordained 10/17/1943 in Florida Presbytery, to preach at Springfield PC in Panama City, FL [1943-44]. During World War II he served as a US Army Chaplain [1944-1947] in Belgium and Central Europe.

Afterward, he then studied at Central Pacific College {UPCUSA} [1947-48] and transferred to the northern denomination, the United Presbyterian Church, USA.

He taught as a professor at the Stuart Robinson School in Blackey, KY [1948], which was a Presbyterian Mission School {PCUS} established in 1913 that operated as a co-educational boarding school for grades 1-12. The school closed in 1957 and the 16 acre campus is now used as the Calvary Camp Retreat Center.

From there he went to Baton Rouge PC in LA [1949-51] before coming to Waxhaw as the pastor here and at Banks PC [1951-53]. He left Waxhaw in 1953 and was dismissed to the Fellowship of Independent Evangelical Churches on 8/25/1953. It had been formed in 1922 as a reformed, yet independent organization of churches. Their focus was on mission work. It is primarily a British organization.

He evidently came back to the PCUS, because he had his 'authority withdrawn' according to BCO 111-3 on 4/24/1973 in Enoree Presbytery.

The Potters served as missionaries in Mexico, Columbia, French West Indes and Central America. After 1973 they became Baptists and taught in schools, ending up in Austin, TX. He died 1/13/2001 in Austin and is buried next to his wife [d. 2004] in the Oaklawn Memorial Cemetery in Athens, TX.

Let us thank God for his ministry among us!

The Ministers of Waxhaw Presbyterian Church- #18

The 18th minister to serve Waxhaw Presbyterian Church was **Orion William Perrell**. He was the son of Walter Luther Perrell and Martha Zeta Swearington of Concord, NC and was born 5/4/1908, the 5th child.

He attended Davidson College [1929-33, BS] and Union Seminary [1933-36, BD]. After graduation he was licensed to preach 9/15/1936 and ordained 10/25/1936 by Lexington Presbytery.

Orion William Perrell in 1990

He began ministry as the pastor of Williamsville PC & Rocky Springs PC in VA [1936-40]. While he was there he met and married Charlotte Mame Rolston 12/28/1937. They had two children: Orion Rolston Perrell and Mary Zeta Perrell [who died earlier this year, June 26th].

The family moved to the Gate City PC and Rockview PC in Nicklesville, VA [1940-41], NC and Stoney Creek PC. Afterward, he transferred to the UPCUSA church 1/29/1947--8/30/1949 when he returned to Lexington Presbytery to pastor Collierstown PC (VA) [1949-55].

On 8/1/1955 Rev. Perrell came to Waxhaw Presbyterian Church for exactly 8 years. During his time here, new members were brought into the faith each year: 1955: 17; 1956: 4; 1957: 7; 1958: 6; 1959: 6; 1960: 3 [including Margaret Steele]; 1961: 4; 1962: 5; 1963:

5, for a total of 58 new members. There were 37 losses during the same period: 5 to death, 6 to the inactive roll and 26 transfers. From Waxhaw, Rev. Perrell went to El Bethel PC in Leakesville, NC [1963-67] and then to Effingham PC in SC [1967-73].

He retired from active pastoring on his 65th birthday, 5/4/1973 in Pee Dee Presbytery. Rev. Perrell died in Florence, SC 2/15/2002 and is buried next to his wife in the Mount Hope Cemetery in Florence, SC.

Let us give thanks to God for his work in the kingdom and at Waxhaw.

A snowy scene of the church in earlier days.

The Ministers of Waxhaw Presbyterian Church- #19

The 19th minister to serve Waxhaw Presbyterian Church was **William Dennis Morton, III**. He was born 2/12/1914 in Ripley, MS, the son of Rev. Henry Flournoy Morton and Elizabeth Lucile Hassell. His father [1886-1920], was a Presbyterian Minister as well, and married Elizabeth on 1/2/1913 in Richmond, VA. He died at the age of 27 in Rocky Mount, NC when Dennis was only six. His grandfather, William Dennis Morton, Sr. [1843-1918], was also a Presbyterian minister.

Dennis Morton went to Davidson College [1932-36] and received an A.B. before advancing to Union Theological Seminary [1946-50], with a B.Div.

William Dennis Morton Rev. Morton married Jane Katherine Chamblee 8/12/1954 in Montreat, NC with the service performed by Rev. James M. McChessey, Jr. They had two children: Katherine Rochet Morton and William Dennis Morton, IV.

Rev. Morton was ordained 5/22/1951 by Albemarle Presbytery and was installed in the Bethany PC in Wilson, NC and the Boyd Memorial PC in Greenville, NC [1951-57]. He then was the pastor of Boyd Memorial, Bethel PC and Johnson Memorial PC [1957-64].

On June 1, 1964 the Mortons moved to Waxhaw as Rev. Morton was installed as the pastor of Waxhaw Presbyterian Church. He remained here until 12/31/1978.

On 3/31/1979 he was honorably retired by Mecklenburg Presbytery.

Rev. Morton was the longest serving minister at Waxhaw at 14 years and 7 months. During his ministry here 73 new members were brought into the fellowship, with 30 of them by Profession of Faith. They included Jane McNeely, Susan Steele and Billy Steele.

Ironically, 73 also left the membership during the same period. 11 of them died, 34 transferred to other churches and the remaining 28 were removed to the inactive list.

Rev. Morton died 4/1/1998 and is buried next to his wife in the Silver Brook Cemetery in Anderson, SC.

Let us give thanks to God for his labor in the kingdom of God.

The Ministers of Waxhaw Presbyterian Church- #20

The 20th minister to serve Waxhaw Presbyterian Church was **Clive Franklin Jacks, Junior**. He was born 3/16/1932 in Atlanta, GA to Clive Franklin Jacks, Sr. and Elizabeth Catherine George.

He was educated in Decatur, GA and graduated from Emory University [1948-52] and Columbia Theological Seminary [1952-55, BD]. He was licensed to preach 9/27/1955 and ordained 11/6/1955 by Atlanta Presbytery. He continued as an instructor at Columbia [1955-57].

He then attended Union Theological Seminary, NY [1957-60, ThD]. He continued as a visiting lecturer at Bangor Theological Seminary, ME [1962-64] and then was an associate professor at Spalding College, KY [1965-69].

Clive Franklin Jacks

Rev. Jacks continued teaching as an associate professor at Queens College, NC [1969-74] and then was a Teacher-at-large [1974-76].

His first pastorate was at the Stephenson PC in Indian Trail, NC [1976-1979], followed by Waxhaw PC [1/1/1979-10/31/1986], a period of 7 years and 10 months. During his pastorate there were 22 additions and 23 losses [3 deaths, 4 removed to the inactive list and 16 out-of-town transfers].

Rev. Jacks is retired and living in Stone Mountain, GA. He is our oldest surviving, full pastor at 83⅔ years of age, tomorrow! {Rev.

55

Aaronson is the oldest interim supply at 88 years and 2 months today.} Rev. Jacks has one son, Timothy Franklin Jacks. Dr. Jacks is also found in the *Who's Who in Religion, 1975-1977.*

Clive F. Jacks, Jr.
Associate Professor of Religion

from a Queens College annual

Let us give thanks to God for his teaching and pastoral ministry that has been rendered throughout the latter half of the 20th Century.

The Ministers of Waxhaw Presbyterian Church- #21

The 21st minister to serve Waxhaw Presbyterian Church was **Charles Edwin Kirkpatrick**. He was born 6/11/1922 in Lillington, NC, the son of Rev. Gurdon Foster Kirkpatrick [1886-1956] and Katie Dian McNeill. Being a 'son of the manse' must have prepared him for the ministry as he would see his own father carrying on the work of the Lord. He was the grandson of Rev. Robert McKemie

Rev. Charles Edwin Kirkpatrick, Sr.

Kirkpatrick [1848-1888], the nephew of Rev. Robert Foster Kirkpatrick [1877-1949] and the 1st cousin of Rev. Robert White Kirkpatrick [1908-1989]. These <u>five</u> Kirkpatricks served many North Carolina churches.

He was the grandson of Rev. Robert McKemie Kirkpatrick [1848-1888], the nephew of Rev. Robert Foster Kirkpatrick [1877-1949] and the 1st cousin of Rev. Robert White Kirkpatrick [1908-1989]. These <u>five</u> Kirkpatricks served many North Carolina churches.

Rev. Charles Edwin Kirkpatrick attended Presbyterian Junior College [1939-41] in Maxton, NC and then entered the Navy's apprentice school for shipbuilding [1941-44] and then the US Navy Reserves [1944-46].

After the war he then graduated from Maryville College, TN [1946-48, AB] and continued to Columbia Theological Seminary [1948-51,

M.Div.]. He was licensed to preach 4/19/51 and ordained 7/1/1951 by Bethel Presbytery, SC.

His first pastorates were at McConnells PC, SC & Zion PC in Lowrys, SC [1951-57], followed by 1st PC Forest City, NC [1957-66] and the McPherson PC in Fayetteville [1966-77]. He then went to Locust PC [1977-87] before coming to Waxhaw PC [2/1/1987- 9/1/1991] as a Stated Supply.

Rev. Kirkpatrick married Dorothy Sue Lemmon in Newport News, VA 8/28/1945 while in the Navy and they had 5 children: Dorothy Sue, Amy Dian, Charles Edwin Jr., Robert Harvey and William Lemmon.

Rev. Kirkpatrick died 12/7/2011, while living in the High Point Retirement Center in High Point, NC. The Kirkpatricks are buried in the Forest Lawn East Cemetery in Weddington, NC.

Let us give thanks to God for his ministry in Waxhaw!

The Ministers of Waxhaw Presbyterian Church- #22

The 22st minister to serve Waxhaw Presbyterian Church was **Deneise Carol Deter-Liss**. She was born 5/24/1956 in Charlottesville, VA to James Wright Deter and Sue Carol Foster. He was an estate planner and she was a music teacher. Rev. Deter-Liss was educated at the Univ. of Virginia [1978-1979], graduating from Denison University in Ohio. She then entered Union Theological Seminary in Richmond, VA and graduated from there in 1984.

Rev. Deter-Liss began as a chaplain and instructor at Queens College [1985-1987] and was ordained 3/9/1986 by the Charlotte Presbytery. Her first pastorate was as associate pastor at First PC, Albemarle, NC [1987-89]. She then began to work with the Pastoral Counseling Center in Charlotte [1990-2002, affiliated with the AAPC].

Deneise Deter-Liss

But during that time she continue to minister in the local church, with Waxhaw PC being next [9/1/1991-6/30/1992]. As an Interim Supply her 10-month ministry brought 17 people into the church, with only one death during the same period.

Afterward, she continued to work in counseling and moved to the Winston-Salem area to continue this work. Her membership transferred to Salem Presbytery and she worked in a church in Ashe Co., NC. She married David Liss in 2002, came back to Charlotte Presbytery [2007] and transferred again to Western NC Presbytery when she became the pastor of Glendale Springs PC [2008-11]. She them move to Long Creek PC in Kings Mountain [2011-14] and then retired in late 2014.

Currently, she lives with her husband and dogs in Bessemer City, NC and continues with occasional supply work and counselling.

Let us give thanks to God for her ministry among us and in the kingdom of God!

The Ministers of Waxhaw Presbyterian Church- #23

The 23rd minister to serve Waxhaw Presbyterian Church was **Katherine Dall Campbell.** She was born 6/29/1956 to Harry Eugene & Rose Mildred Dall in Omaha, NE. Harry was a clerk in his brother's drug store and later for the local railroad.

Kathy Campbell
1992

After growing up in Nebraska, Kathy went to Warren Wilson College [1974-77 (BA in History & Political Science)] and remained there as a Campus Chaplain [1977-83].

She met and married Karl Campbell in [6-21-1980] of Asheville, a history teacher at the Asheville School.

Kathy went to Duke Divinity School [83-87, M.Div.] and was the campus chaplain while there. After graduation, she was ordained 10-31-1987 in the Eastern Virginia Presbytery, moving to Virginia to be the chaplain at Mary Washington College [1987-92] and then UNCC [1992-95]. Karl was an Adjunct Professor of History there [1992-93].

During this time Kathy was the Interim Supply at Waxhaw [11/1/1992-9/30/1993]. They expressed many fond memories of Waxhaw while they were here 23 years ago!

Karl finished his PhD at UNC in 1995 and they moved to Misenheimer, NC at Pheiffer College, where he taught and she ministered [1996-97].

In 1997 they made a big move to the mountains of North Carolina and settled in the Banner Elk area. Kathy was the chaplain of Lees-McRae College [1997-2009] and an interim supply at the Fletcher PC [1998-99]. Karl has been Professor of History at Appalachian since 1997. Kathy also served as an interim supply at the Newland PC [2000-01]. She is now the Pastor at Crossnore PC, NC [6/1/2009ff].

She enjoys community building with Habitat for Humanity and community building relationships. For enjoyment she hikes, reads and cooks. Kathy and Karl have one child, Joanna.

Let us give thanks to God for her ministry to God's people.

The Ministers of Waxhaw Presbyterian Church- #24

The 24th minister to serve Waxhaw Presbyterian Church was **Jane Flowe Brawley (Fobel).** Jane was born in the Robinson PC community on 2/12/1954 to Victor Howard Brawley and Annie Mae Flowe. She went to Independence High School [1972] and Agnes Scott College with a BA in Bible and Religion [1976].

She came 'Under the Care' of Mecklenburg Presbytery 12/1975 along with the three Carriker brothers and other Charlotte area ministers. Jane attended Union Theological Seminary in Richmond, VA, completing one year of Clinical Pastoral Education at the Medical College of Richmond and graduated with a D. Min. in 1980. She was then ordained 9/23/1980 by Mecklenburg Presbytery.

Rev. Jane Brawley Foble in Waxhaw

Her church service began with Troy UPC [NC] [1981-84] before going back to school at Harvard University, graduating in 1985 with a Masters in Theology. She then became an Associate Pastor at Charlotte's First PC [1985-91]. While there, she married Mark Joseph Fobel 3/21/1987. Their children are Peter and Lydia.

The next work that Rev. Fobel completed was at Newell PC [1991-93] as an Interim Pastor.

Jane came to Waxhaw PC 10/24/1993 and remained until 5/31/1994. She was the last of the three, one-year Interim Supply ministers that encouraged the people of Waxhaw between Rev. Jacks and Rev. Gerstenmier, who began one month after Rev. Fobel left. But she was an Interim Pastor at one more church: East PC [1994-95].

She has served Mecklenburg & Charlotte Presbytery churches her entire career. In March 1997 she accepted a position at Sardis PC as Associate Pastor and has been there almost 20 years now.

We thank God for her ministry in our midst and pray for her continued time at Sardis.

The Ministers of Waxhaw Presbyterian Church- #25

The 25th minister to serve Waxhaw Presbyterian Church was **John David Gerstenmier**. John was born November 15, 1948 in Newark, New Jersey to Charles Stanley Gerstenmier and Mae Frances Rodger.

John David Gerstenmier

He is a graduate of the College of New Jersey in Trenton, with a BA Mathematics Education and a Master of Education. His focus was in Student Personnel & Counseling. After graduation he join the United States Marine Corp [1971-78] and served primarily at the Picatinny Arsenal in Dover, NJ.

While in the service he also taught Mathematics and Science [1971-81]. John met Lynn Marie Eisinger in his home church, Union Hill PC, Denville, NJ. They were married on 7/2/77.

After teaching, John worked in computer sales management [1981-85] prior to his enrollment at Princeton Seminary in [1985-87]. He graduated with a M.Div. in Pastoral Counseling and began his ministry serving as the pastor of Milton PC [PA] [8/1987-5/1994]. He was ordained on 8/17/1987 by Newton Presbytery.

From Pennsylvania, the Gerstenmiers came to Waxhaw on 6/1/1994. They came with David [1981], Adam [1983] and Philip [1988], ages 13, 11 and 6. While here John oversaw the transition of the church to its new location with the implementation of the Child Development Center.

Presbytery Committee to redevelop!

The Third Sanctuary under construction

[above] the front of the church
[below] an aerial view of the property

His ministry in Waxhaw ended 6/30/2004 when he accepted a call to minister at the Salem/Pageland PC in Pageland, SC where he labored until 5/2008.

In that month his ministry focused on the Smart Start Rowan program, a validated ministry by Charlotte Presbytery, located in Salisbury, NC.

In 6/2013 he accepted a call as an Interim Supply at Bethany PC in Union Co., NC, where he currently serves today.

The Gerstenmiers have 7 grandchildren and reside in their home that was built in 1995. They are still a vital part of the community and the ministry that is offered here.

The third sanctuary!

We thank God for their service in ministry at Waxhaw PC and pray for their continued service and health!

The Ministers of Waxhaw Presbyterian Church- #26

The 26th minister of Waxhaw Presbyterian Church is **David Richard Aaronson.** Rev. Aaronson was born 9/15/1927 in Columbus, NJ to Edward S. Aaronson and Margaret G. Lewis. His parents were farmers in the present Burlington County, NJ and the farm house was about 12 miles south of Trenton. Rev. Aaronson attended Wheaton

Rev. Aaronson & carolers!

College [BA, Sociology, 1948] and Princeton Seminary [BD, 1951]. He was ordained after graduation on 5/21/1951 by Newton Presbytery.

He served three churches:
Harmony PC [1951-60, Phillipsburg, NJ],
Calvary PC [1960-71, Newburgh, NY] and
Sparta First PC [1971-98, Sparta, NJ],
for 47 years, all in New Jersey.

On 10/13/1992 he retired from full-time ministry and was elected as Pastor Emeritus at the Sparta PC.

Rev. Aaronson was married to Sue Ruth Poinsett [1926-2006] and they had three children: Kathy, Karen and Kevin. He now has five grandchildren to his family.

The Aaronson family moved to Charlotte in 1998. Rev. Aaronson began serving as a Parish Associate at Sardis PC [1998-2002] before serving in Union County. He then served for 1 year at Altan and Bethany Presbyterian Churches [2004-05] before coming to Waxhaw Presbyterian Church 1/31/2006-6/30/2006. While here, he worked with church leaders to move toward a spirit of unity in preparation to call a new pastor. This was accomplished 7/1/2006 when Rev. Carriker began his ministry here.

After leaving Waxhaw PC, Rev. Aaronson served only Altan PC for 2 years [2006-08] and again for a few months in 2009. At that point health issues led him to fully retire from ministry.

Rev. Aaronson is known as a healing and enriching pastor. His service here and in this presbytery are held in high esteem and for this, we give thanks to God for his ministry!

The Ministers of Waxhaw Presbyterian Church- #27

The 27th minister of Waxhaw Presbyterian Church is **The Reverend Doctor Samuel David Carriker, Senior.** He was born in Charlotte, NC July 23, 1951 to John A. and Bernie Mull Carriker, Jr. His brothers are John, III, Tim and Richard. He was baptized at Eastminster Presbyterian Church October 28, 1951 where his grandfather, The Rev. John A. Carriker, Sr., was the Pastor and the church sat on the hill above the old Coliseum and auditorium on Independence Blvd.

Rev. John A. Carriker, Sr., with Richard Carriker [left], **Rev. Dr. Tim Carriker** [center] **& Rev. Dr. David Carriker**

Faith began in his life with the nurturing of a family committed in faith to Jesus Christ. On 4/19/1962 Rev. Carriker made a confession of faith in Jesus Christ at Westminster PC under the leadership of Rev. I. Howard Chadwick. It was at Westminster that he joined the Youth Group.

In August of 1968, while staying with his grandparents in Montreat, NC, he made a recommitment to Christ through a Youth Conference message that just happened to be given by the Rev. Billy Graham. During the prayer time, Rev. Graham led David and 11 other boys in prayer in an upper room and the call of God became a seed of faith in his life.

In the following year Rev. Carriker entered Central Piedmont Community College [1969-71] and later transferred to the University of North Carolina at Charlotte [1971-75]. About the same time the

Carriker family moved to the Sardis Presbyterian Church area and became active there. After working with the local church youth, at The Salt Cellar, a community coffeehouse and in local fellowship groups he became involved in the early formation of the Christian Fellowship at UNCC. There he felt called into the gospel ministry after seeing and understanding the preparation God had started in his life.

Rev. Carriker graduated from UNCC in 1975 with a BA in Geography and Earth Science and was taken under the care of Mecklenburg Presbytery in August of 1975 along with brothers Tim and Richard. In the following month he continued to Decatur, GA where he was accepted into Columbia Theological Seminary. While in seminary he focused on Apologetics, Hebrew and Biblical Studies.

For seminary-sponsored summer ministries, Rev. Carriker served three churches in three areas as summer intern:
1) general ministry at Marion PC [SC] in 1976,
2) Bible Study & Youth work at Sugaw Creek PC in 1977, and
3) Retreats, Vacation Bible Schools, children's ministry and Senior work at Decatur PC [GA] in 1978, where he held the title "Minister of Recreation." It was fun! He graduated later that year [Master of Divinity 1978].

Rev. Carriker was ordained March 10, 1979 at his first call where he was pastor to McLean PC & Rourk PC [1979-85] in Ellerbe, NC. All four of the children were born there: Dave [1979], Ashleigh [1981], Jonathan [1982] and Rebekah [1984]. While there, Rev. Carriker was a Scoutmaster, organizer of the local CropWalk, the vice-president of the National Railroad Museum and he began writing.

Rev. Carriker's third church was Union PC in Gastonia, NC [1986-1993] where continuing education began in Evangelism and Church growth. In 1993 he began work on his doctorate, on Peter's sermon in Acts 2.

Soon after, the Carrikers moved to Lynnhaven PC in Virginia Beach, VA [1994-97]. With a military membership [85% active or retired] a different challenge was exciting in Virginia. Different opportunities with Habitat for Humanity, the local Shelter and small fellowship groups offered new perspectives of ministry. New friendships were established and for the first time the Carolina Carrikers had the accent in Tidewater Virginia! Rev. Carriker's fifth church was Third Creek PC in Cleveland, NC [1998-2006], a 250 year old church which became a model for his doctorate. His work concluded in the area of Church Renewal and Revitalization [Doctor of Ministry, 2001] at the State's 5th oldest Presbyterian Church. He also went to the Presbytery's orphanage in China as Chair of the Presbytery's Worldwide Ministries Cluster.

The three living full-time pastors:
Carriker, Gerstenmier and Jacks
at Waxhaw First Presbyterian Church

Today, his children live in former towns where he ministered: Dave in Cleveland, Bekah & Ben Motley in nearby Linwood and Jon & Lauren Carriker in Ellerbe. Ashleigh is a traveling Radiographer, currently at a hospital in Sacremento, CA.

Now Rev. Carriker has been in Waxhaw, NC for 10 years at Waxhaw Presbyterian Church where God has led him. Through highs and lows the fellowship here is rich in grace. There are not enough words to describe the love, grace and caring demeanor of the people of this church. In thankfulness for God's providence and grace, His love to us is shown through Jesus Christ.

Rev. Carriker became a Stated Supply Pastor at Waxhaw since March

1, 2011. Retirement soon followed March 10, 2014, thirty-five years after beginning ordained ministry, yet he still serves as stated supply for half-time services.

On 10/25/2015 David Carriker & Karen Greer were married at the church. David & Karen are grateful for the life, love and support here and they call this "home!"

Robert Ney McNeely, II
'my friend' and a lay
Pastor to the community

We give thanks for this ministry and work here.

Ministers *From* the Church

The Ministers *From* Waxhaw Presbyterian Church- #1

Robert Lee Walkup was born in the Waxhaw Community. He and his brother, John L. Walkup, were sons of Samuel H. & Eleanor Steele Walkup. When Waxhaw PC welcomed its 5th minister, Rev. Hugh Hoon, his evangelistic preaching brought some of the Walkups to our church. Robert's older brother, John L., made a profession of faith 3/25/1897, along with his wife, Susan.

Robert became a Christian at Waxhaw PC on 9/26/1901, under the preaching of Rev. John Dixon. Robert was born 9/3/1880 in Waxhaw and was called of God to Christian service in 4/16/1902 when he came under the care of Mecklenburg Presbytery to begin training.

Robert Lee Walkup was already from a dynasty of Walkup ministers. The Walkups [Wauchobe] came to the Staunton, VA area. His great grandfather, Israel, was the first to be born in America, in the Waxhaw Settlement of SC. Israel's grandfather, Samuel, was the first to die in America.

Robert went to school at PCSC and Southwestern Pres. College [1903-07] and graduated with a B.Ph., before finishing at their divinity school. He was ordained in 1907 by Louisiana Presbytery and was pastor at Hoyte Memorial PC and Unity PC [1907-11] in Mississippi, where he married [#1] Clara Robinson in 1910. She died within a year in childbirth.

He then married Margaret Caldwell in 1913 [see article] while at Brookhaven PC. He was the secretary of Missions & Sunday Schools for the Synod of Miss. [1914-15]. For four years, Robert Lee Walkup served the Southern Presbyterian Church in Montreat, NC as the secretary of the Stewardship Committee [1915-18].

Dec 18, 1913- AN INTERESTING WEDDING

Among the many fair daughters of Senatobia that have been given to assume the holy vows of marriage not one has shone with more purity or radiant loveliness than did MARGARET CALDWELL, as she plighted her eternal troth to that splendid young man Rev. ROBERT LEE WALKUP of North Carolina. Mr. WALKUP is prominently known as

Synodical Evangelist and Secretary of Home Missions in the State of Miss. MARGARET is the first born daughter of Mr. & Mrs. J. W. CALDWELL. The audience assembled in the Presbyterian Church, where she from early childhood has been faithful and active in good works and where before her the Grandfather Caldwell, his sons and Grandson have preached. The nuptial music was rendered by Mrs. IRVER SALMON and Mr. HARRY TUCKER. Ring bearer was Miss ISABEL CHAPMAN; maid of honor was Miss AGNES PERKINS, cousin of the bride. The service was spoken by Dr. S. C. CALDWELL, uncle of the bride and was assisted by Rev. W. W. PATTON of Pontotoc.

-- Tate County Democrat

He went on a trip back to MS to visit his in-laws and died after a brief illness at age 38.

There are no known photographs of Rev. Walkup among his descendants. His son, Rev. Robert Harvey Walkup was born in Jackson, MS and served churches in that area. His brother, William, had two sons who were ordained as well: Rev. John Walkup in Kings Mt. Presbytery & Rev. James Walkup in Orange Presbytery. Both men were raised in Tirzah.

Death of Rev. R. L. Walkup.

Rev. R. L. Walkup of Montreat, N. C., died at Centerville, Miss., Tuesday evening, Nov. 26, while on a visit with his wife and children to Mrs. Walkup's people, and also for the purpose of appearing before the Synod of Mississippi in behalf of the Southern General Assembly's Stewardship Committee.

Mr. Walkup was born in Union county Sept. ?, 1880. He was the youngest son of the late Mr. and Mrs. S. H. Walkup. He is survived by his wife and two sons, twins, about four years old. Mr. Walkup was first married to Miss Clara Robinson of Mississippi who died about one year after their marriage, nearly eight years ago. His second marriage was to Miss Margaret Caldwell of Miss. He is also survived by the following brothers and sisters: Messrs. J. L. and W. S. Walkup, Mrs. R. N. Nisbet, Mrs. G. A. McCain, Mrs. R. J. Belk, Mrs. J. W. Craig, and Mrs. R. C. Ratchford. He was greatly loved and therefore will be sorely missed by his family and friends, also the Southern Presbyterian church will suffer a distinct loss, as he was a very active and efficient worker, and faithful minister. For the last four or five years he has been the efficient secretary of the Assembly's Stewardship Committee. His place will be hard to fill, for there are comparatively few who have such energy and determination as had he and few who have the capacity and ability for organizing, handling men, and directing a great work for the church.— R. N. Nisbet.

Monroe Journal 11/29/1918

Rev. Robert Lee Walkup's great uncle, Rev. Samuel Waucobe [kept the old spelling], was a minister in Virginia before the Civil War. He had a son, Rev. Joseph Walker Waucobe, who was ordained in VA and died in Columbia, SC. He had 3 sons that were ordained: Rev. Joseph [VA], Rev. Arthur [WV], Rev. William [Concord Presbytery], and 2 daughters who married NC ministers: Mary Walkup *Rhea* and Katherine Walkup *Read*, both serving in the mountains.

That is **one** minister who came out of our church, three of his descendants, one great uncle, one uncle, three cousins, and two cousins-in-law,

ALL ministers in the old Presbyterian Church, US.

79

The Walkups of America
{with the Vaucobs/Wauchopes}
By S. David Carriker, D.Min., 2015

CODES

Members of Waxhaw PC
[red border]

Waxhaw Walkup ministers
[green shading]

Virginia Wauchope ministers
[blue shading]

☆ served in the
Carolinas

Samuel Vachub Sr.
b: 1636 in Fergus, Ireland
d: Aft. 1666 in Fergus, Ireland

?
b: Bef. 1650
d: Aft. 1666

Samuel Vachub Jr.
b: 1666 in Fergus, Ireland
d: Aft. 1695 in Fergus, Ireland

Nancy Agnes Alexander
b: 1669 in Fergus, Ireland
d: Aft. 1695 in Fergus, Ireland

Samuel Vachub III [Pioneer]
b: 1695 in Fergus, Cross Roads, Ireland
d: 1762 in Lexington, VA

Nancy Agnes Alexander
b: 1690 in Carrick Fergus, Ireland
d: 1740 in Staunton, VA

WAXHAW, SC/NC Walkups

Capt. James Alexander
Walkup   [Pioneer]
b: Nov 15, 1724 in Carrick Fergus, Ireland
d: Feb 01, 1796 in Waxhaw Settlement, SC;
[formerly, Mecklenburg Co. NC]

Margaret Nancy Pickens
b: Dec 05, 1740 in Augusta, VA
d: Dec 22, 1793 in Waxhaw Settlement, SC;
[formerly, Mecklenburg Co., NC]

VIRGINIA Wauchopes

John Arthur Wauchope
b: 1734 in Lancaster Co. PA
d: 1834 in Rockbridge, VA

Elizabeth Lockridge
b: Abt. 1750
d: Bef. 1797 in Rockbridge Co., VA

80

The Walkups of the Carolinas
By S. David Carriker, D.Min., 2015

Capt. James Alexander Walkup [Pioneer]
b: Nov 15, 1724 in Carrick Fergus, Ireland
d: Feb 01, 1798 in Waxhaw Settlement, SC;
[formerly, Mecklenburg Co., NC]

Margaret Nancy Pickens
b: Dec 05, 1740 in Augusta, VA
d: Dec 22, 1793 in Waxhaw Settlement, SC;
[formerly, Mecklenburg Co., NC]

Israel Pickens Walkup
b: Sep 17, 1768 in Waxhaw Settlement, SC;
[formerly, Mecklenburg Co., NC]
d: Oct 06, 1822 in Union Co., NC

Margaret Peggy Morrow
b: Sep 11, 1776 in Waxhaw, NC; [formerly,
Mecklenburg Co., NC]
d: Sep 01, 1829 in Waxhaw, NC; [formerly,
Mecklenburg Co., NC]

Samuel Pickens Walkup
b: Jan 30, 1799 in Waxhaw Settlement, SC;
[formerly, Mecklenburg Co., NC]
d: Jul 16, 1885 in Jackson Tp, Union Co., NC

Martha Matilda Craig
b: 1805 in Union Co., NC; [formerly,
Mecklenburg Co., NC]
d: 1844 in Union Co., NC

Samuel Harvey Walkup
b: Dec 04, 1838 in Union Co. NC; [formerly,
Mecklenburg Co., NC]
d: May 16, 1892 in Union Co., NC

Eleanor Jane Steele
b: Sep 30, 1841 in Union Co., NC
d: Dec 02, 1915 in Union Co., NC

Robert Lee Walkup ☆
b: Sep 03, 1880 in Waxhaw, NC
d: Nov 26, 1916 in Centerville, MS

Margaret Caldwell
b: Aug 10, 1882 in Senatobia, MS
d: Jul 26, 1921 in Senatobia, MS

John Harper Walkup Sr
b: Jan 20, 1915 in Senatobia, MS
d: Mar 30, 1993 in Danville, KY; Chemistry Prof.
at Centre College

Robert Harvey Walkup MS
d: Jan 20, 1915 in Senatobia, MS
d: Apr 23, 1992 in Danville, KY

Mayme Stover
b: Feb 16, 1876 in South Carolina
d: Sep 24, 1926 in Jackson Tsp., Union Co., NC

John Samuel Walkup ☆
b: May 09, 1916 in Waxhaw, NC
d: Dec 24, 2002 in Sumter, SC - Age 86

William Samuel Walkup
b: May 12, 1878 in Waxhaw, NC
d: Nov 20, 1949 in Monroe, NC

James William Stover Walkup ☆
b: Sep 09, 1909 in Waxhaw, NC
d: Jan 03, 1998 in Charlotte, NC

The Wauchopes of Virginia
By S. David Carriker, D.Min., 2015

John Arthur Wauchope
b 1734 in Lancaster Co, PA
d 1834 in Rockbridge, VA

Elizabeth Lockridge
b Abt. 1759
d Bef. 1797 in Rockbridge Co., VA

Samuel Wauchope   VA
b Feb 11, 1737 in Rockbridge, VA
d May 14, 1802 in Rockbridge, VA

Maria Todd Houston
b May 23, 1798 in Rockbridge, VA
d Nov 29, 1875 in Rockbridge, VA

Rev Joseph Walker Wauchope ☆
b Dec 28, 1826 in Natural Bridge, VA
d Dec 21, 1901 in Carlinville, SC

Katherine Ann "Kate" Kendrick
b Mar 06, 1845 in Strasburg, VA
d Jul 08, 1925 in Somerville, TN, Age 80

Joseph Ailiene Wauchope   VA
b 1873 in Amherst, VA
d.

Arthur Douglas Wauchope ☆
b Jul 11, 1871 in Sweet Bridge, VA
d Mar 15, 1874 in Kansas, LA

William Crawford Wauchope ☆
b Sep 01, 1880 in Hampshire, TN
d Jul 23, 1975 in Concord, NC

Mary Armstrong Wauchope ☆
b Jul 25, 1884 in West Virginia
d May 08, 1948 in Somerville, TN

Alfred Long Rhea ☆
b Dec 05, 1871 in Somerville, TN
d Jul 21, 1923 in Somerville, TN

Katharine Rutherford Wauchope
b Apr 19, 1887 in Natural Bridge, VA
d Nov 19, 1957 in Norman, OK

Rev John Leighton Read ☆
b Sep 14, 1879 in Paris, TX
d Oct 02, 1959 in Norman, OK, Age 80

Katherine Rochet Morton was born in Greenville, NC 5/11/1955, the daughter of Rev. William Dennis Morton & Jane Cameron Chamblee. Being of child of the manse, it was only a matter of time before she would make her way to Waxhaw, NC as a young nine year old. While her parents were here 6/1/1964-12/31/1978, Katherine went through school and graduated from Parkwood Senior High in1973.

Katherine Rochet Morton

She continued her education at Davidson College [BA, 1977] and Union Theological Seminary & Presbyterian School of Christian Education [D.Min. 1981]. While in seminary, she did some mission work in South Korea.

She was ordained in Norfolk Presbytery and began serving in Groves Memorial PC in Hayes, VA 10/1981-5/1984. While there [5/1982] she married Mark Achtemeier, the son of Dr. Elizabeth & Paul Achtemeier.

From 1984-2002 they had three children, Rachel, Sarah & Josh while she continued with pulpit supply, Presbytery work and staying busy in ministry. Katherine & Mark now have three grandchildren, 2, 14 and 21 months of age. Rachel is also an Associate Pastor in New Jersey, so the ministry continues through many generations! In 2002 Katherine became the Temporary Supply at Dubuque First PC in Iowa and became the full pastor in 2003. She continues to serve there to this day. We give thanks to God for his call to Katherine Morton Achtemeier in Iowa.

Appendices

	Ministerial Service at Waxhaw Presbyterian Church				
Order	Minister	Type	Ordained	Beginning	Ending
1	Robinson, Charles Wilson Harris	Supply	1879/10/24	1888/10/19	1890/08/31
2	McLees, John Logan	Supply	1885/10/30	1888/10/19	1889/10/31
3	Dixon, Henderson Makemie	Supply	1888/00/00	1891/03/01	1895/02/01
4	Boggs, William Kennedy	Pastor	1862/00/00	1895/10/01	1896/10/09
5	Hoon, Hugh William	Pastor	1897/04/22	1897/03/01	1901/01/31
6	Dixon, John Howie	Pastor	1884/12/04	1901/04/01	1905/10/31
7	McKinstry, John Logan	Pastor	1888/10/19	1906/11/01	1908/10/31
8	Pace, George Thomas	Supply	1900/00/00	1910/01/01	1910/10/16
9	Robertson, Charles Edward	Pastor	1894/09/13	1911/01/01	1918/07/14
10	Thompson, George Brazier	Pastor	1907/10/06	1919/12/31	1923/05/01
11	Kingsley, Charles Eugene	Pastor	1904/00/00	1924/05/01	1926/03/02
12	Grier, Thomas Franklin	Supply	1927/00/00	1927/10/01	1927/11/06
13	White, Carlton Emory	Supply	1909/03/28	1928/04/01	1930/04/30
14	Cocks, James Frazer	Supply	1904/05/11	1930/05/01	1930/09/21
15	Wiley, Ewell Van Buren	Pastor	1930/07/15	1934/10/21	1948/07/15
16	Tackett, Jack Robert	Pastor	1925/10/00	1949/03/01	1950/06/30
17	Potter, Charles Wayne	Pastor	1943/10/17	1951/04/01	1953/08/30
18	Perrell, Orion William	Pastor	1936/10/25	1955/08/01	1963/08/01
19	Morton, William Dennis, III	Pastor	1951/05/22	1964/06/01	1978/12/31
20	Jacks, Clive Franklin, Jr.	Int. Sup./P.	1955/11/06	1979/01/01	1986/10/31
21	Kirkpatrick, Charles Edwin	Int./S. Sup.	1951/07/01	1987/02/01	1991/09/01
22	Rankin, Deneise C. Deter-Liss	Int. Sup.	1986/03/09	1991/09/01	1992/06/30+
23	Campbell, Kathy Dall	Int. Sup.	1987/10/08[1]	1992/11/01	1993/09/30
24	Fobel, Jane Flowe Brawley	Int. Sup.	1980/09/23	1993/10/24	1994/05/31
25	Gerstenmier, John David	Pastor	1987/08/17	1994/06/01	2004/06/30
26	Aaronson, David Richard	Int. Sup.	1950/05/15	2006/01/31	2006/07/01
27	Carriker, Samuel David, Sr.	P./S. Sup.	1979/03/10	2006/07/01	
			[1] most recent ordination		

A Chart of Ministerial Service including ordination and service dates.

Order	Minister	Birth	Death	Age In	Age out	Time Here
	Ministerial Personal Dates, Ages Coming & Going, and Length of Service					
1	Robinson, Charles Wilson Harris	1848/06/25[1]	1938/01/11	40	43	01/10/12
2	McLees, John Logan	1855/05/24	1925/04/21	33	36	01/00/12
3	Dixon, Henderson Makemie	1860/09/18	1937/09/05	31	35	03/11/00
4	Boggs, William Kennedy	1850/10/18	1896/10/09[4]	45	46	01/00/08
5	Hoon, Hugh William	1871/05/27	1916/03/04	26[2]	30[2]	03/11/00
6	Dixon, John Howie	1852/09/01	1919/01/12	49	53	04/07/00
7	McKinstry, John Logan	1878/07/17	1955/02/15	28	30	02/00/00
8	Pace, George Thomas	1865/10/20	1936/06/01	44	44	00/09/15
9	Robertson, Charles Edward	1851/02/16	1942/08/08	57	64	07/06/14
10	Thompson, George Brazier	**1874/01/29**	1944/03/18	45	49	03/05/00
11	Kingsley, Charles Eugene	1860/05/20	1933/07/01	64	66	01/10/02
12	Grier, Thomas Franklin	**1885/10/27**	1965/06/16	41	43	00/01/05[5]
13	White, Carlton Emory	1883/07/24	1947/01/21	45	47	02/01/00
14	Cocks, James Frazer	1871/11/05	1943/08/30	59	62	00/04/20
15	Wiley, Ewell Van Buren	1902/06/13	1956/08/18	32	46	13/08/24
16	Tackett, Jack Robert	1898/06/22	1984/01/15	51	52	01/04/00
17	Potter, Charles Wayne	1918/02/05	2001/01/13	33	35	02/04/30
18	Perrell, Orion William	1908/05/04	2002/02/15	47	55	08/00/00
19	Morton, William Dennis, III	1914/02/12	1998/04/01	50	65	14/07/00[8]
20	Jacks, Clive Franklin, Jr.	1932/03/16	x	48	55	07/10/00
21	Kirkpatrick, Charles Edwin	1922/06/11	2011/12/07[7]	**65**	**69**	04/07/00
22	Rankin, Deneise C. Deter-Liss	1956/05/15	x	35	36	00/10/00
23	Campbell, Kathy Dall	1959/09/01[6]	x	33	34	00/11/00
24	Fobel, Jane Flowe Brawley	1954/02/12	x	39	40	00/07/07
25	Gerstenmier, John David	1948/11/15	x	47	55	10/01/00
26	Aaronson, David Richard	1927/09/15	x	77[3]	79[3]	00/06/00
27	Carriker, Samuel David, Sr.	1951/07/23	x	55	[65+]	10/0/0
	[1] earliest birth		[5] shortest time in service: 35 days			
	[2] youngest age in & out of service		[6] latest birth			
	[3] oldest age in & out of service		[7] latest death			
	[4] earliest death		[8] longest time in service: 14 yrs., 7 mos., 0 days			

Significant dates and numbers of the pastors.

	Ministerial Education and Ordaination				
Order	Minister	Birth	College	Seminary	Ordained In
1	Robinson, Charles Wilson Harris	MS	Davidson	CTS	Louisville
2	McLees, John Logan	SC	Adger	CTS	Mecklenburg
3	Dixon, Henderson Makemie	NC	Davidson[1]	PTS	Charleston
4	Boggs, William Kennedy	SC	[unknown]	CTS	Augusta
5	Hoon, Hugh William	PA	Mari	Pres'y[2]	Mecklenburg
6	Dixon, John Howie	NC	UNC	UTS	Louisville
7	McKinstry, John Logan	TN	SWP	SWPS	Mecklenburg
8	Pace, George Thomas	TN	SWP	UTS	Fayetteville
9	Robertson, Charles Edward	AL	Al. PI	CTS	Enoree
10	Thompson, George Brazier	LA	King	UTS	Durant
11	Kingsley, Charles Eugene	TN	Tusculum	[unknown]	St. Johns
12	Grier, Thomas Franklin	NC	Erskine	ETS/LTS	Mecklenburg
13	White, Carlton Emory	NC	Moravian	MTS	[Moravian]
14	Cocks, James Frazer	ENG	Manitoba[3]	Man.TS[4]	Louisivlle[5]
15	Wiley, Ewell Van Buren	WV	H-Sydney	UTS	Mangum
16	Tackett, Jack Robert	MS	SWP/U.Ms	UTS	Central MS
17	Potter, Charles Wayne	MD	Emory[6]	CTS	Florida
18	Perrell, Orion William	NC	Davidson	UTS	Lexington
19	Morton, William Dennis, III	MS	Davidson	UTS	Albemarle
20	Jacks, Clive Franklin, Jr.	GA	Emory	CTS[7]	Atlanta
21	Kirkpatrick, Charles Edwin	NC	PJC[8]	CTS	Bethel
22	Rankin, Deneise C. Deter-Liss	VA	Denison	UTS	Charlotte
23	Campbell, Kathy Dall	NE	W.Wilson	Duke	Eastern VA
24	Fobel, Jane Flowe Brawley	NC	Agnes S.[9]	UTS	Mecklenburg
25	Gerstenmier, John David	NJ	College NJ	PTS	Newton
26	Aaronson, David Richard	NJ	Wheaton	PTS	Newton
27	Carriker, Samuel David, Sr.	NC	UNCC	CTS	Mecklenburg

Education and ordination of the pastors

[1] Davidson College, University of North Carolina

[2] theological education obtained by training in Presbytery

[3] Manitoba C., U. of Manitoba, Oskalooska C.- Ph.D.; [4] Manitoba TS, Louisville TS, Lane TS; [5] UPCUSA

[6] Presbyterian College, Wheaton College

[7] Columbia Theological Seminary, Union Theological Seminary- NY

[8] Presbyterian Junior College, in Maxton, NC and Maryville College in TN

[9] Agnes Scott College and Harvard University

Note: 4 at **Davidson** College

Note: 8 at **Columbia** Theological Seminary; 9 at **Union** Theological Seminary [VA]

Note: 6 from **Mecklenburg** Presbytery, plus 1 from **Charlotte** Presbytery

School notations for the previous page.

Minister	Born	Age at Death			Bur	Churches & Schools
		Yr	Mo	Dy		
Robinson, Charles Wilson Harris	MS	89	6	17	NC	9
McLees, John Logan	SC	69	10	27	SC	5
Dixon, Henderson Makemie	NC	76	11	18	SC	5
Boggs, William Kennedy	SC	45	11	22	SC	6
Hoon, Hugh William	PA	44	9	7	TX	9
Dixon, John Howie	NC	66	4	11	NC	12
McKinstry, John Logan	TN	76	6	28	TN	7
Pace, George Thomas	TN	70	7	11	NC	8
Robertson, Charles Edward	AL	91	5	22	SC	9
Thompson, George Brazier	LA	70	1	18	KY	11
Kingsley, Charles Eugene	TN	73	1	11	FL	13
Grier, Thomas Franklin	NC	79	7	19	NC	8
White, Carlton Emory	NC	63	5	28	VA	11
Cocks, James Frazer	ENG	71	9	25	FL	15
Wiley, Ewell Van Buren	WV	54	2	5	NC	8
Tackett, Jack Robert	MS	85	6	24	MS	21
Potter, Charles Wayne	MD	82	11	8	TX	7
Perrell, Orion William	NC	93	8	11	SC	9
Morton, William Dennis, III	MS	84	1	17	NC	4
Jacks, Clive Franklin, Jr.	GA	84	4	8	{L}	6
Kirkpatrick, Charles Edwin	NC	89	5	26	NC	7
Rankin, Deneise C. Deter-Liss	VA	60	2	9	{L}	6
Campbell, Kathy Dall	NE	56	10	23	{L}	10
Fobel, Jane Flowe Brawley	NC	62	7	12	{L}	6
Gerstenmier, John David	NJ	67	8	9	{L}	5
Aaronson, David Richard	NJ	89	2	0	{L}	7
Carriker, Samuel David, Sr.	NC	65	3	22	{L}	6
total		1952	161	438		230
ave. age		72	6	5		served

Pastoral ages, average age and churches and schools served.

Conclusion

7 of the 27 ministers were born in North Carolina. One was born in England, one in Pennsylvania, two in New Jersey and the remainder in the South.

The earliest was born 168 years ago [Robinson- 1848]; the latest was born almost 57 years ago [Campbell- 1959].

The earliest ordained was in 1860 [Boggs- 156 years ago] and the latest was in 1987 [Campbell- almost 29 years ago].

The first to die was 120 years ago [Boggs- 1896, the only 19th Century death] and the latest was five years ago [Kirkpatrick- 2011].

The youngest to die was at the age of 44 years, 9 months and 7 days [Hoon] and the oldest was 93 years, 8 months and 11 days [Perrell]. The only one to die while at Waxhaw was Boggs in 1896.

The youngest person to begin serving Waxhaw was at the age of 26 [Hoon] and the oldest was 77 [Aaronson].

The youngest person to end service in Waxhaw was at the age of 30 [McKinstry] and the oldest was 79 [Aaronson].

The longest serving person at Waxhaw was 14 years, 7 months [Morton]. The second longest serving was 13 years, 8 months, 24 days [Wiley] and the third longest was 10 years, 1 month, 1 day [so, far- Carriker on 8/2/2016].

The shortest serving pastorates were Grier [35 days], Cocks [4 mo., 21 days], Aaronson [6 mo.], Fobel [7 mo., 7 days], Pace [9 mo., 15 days], Rankin [10 mo.] and Campbell [11 mo.]. This equates to 7 ministers totaling 4 years, 1 month and 7 days.

"Empty pastorates" [the time between pastorates] have occurred between 22 of the 27 ministers. There was no break prior to the arrival of five pastors. The shortest period of having an 'empty pulpit' was two months and the longest was during the depression: 4 years and 1 month [between Cocks and Wiley {9/21/1930-10/21/1934}].

Four ministers went to Davidson College. Nine ministers went to Union Seminary and eight went to Columbia Seminary. Seven were ordained by Mecklenburg/Charlotte Presbytery.

One came out of the Moravian Church [White], one out of the Associate Reformed Presbyterian Church [Grier], one out of the Canadian Presbyterian Church [Cocks] and one from the Northern church [UPCUSA- Aaronson].

One minister transferred to the Presbyterian Church of America [Tackett] and one to the Independent Fellowship of Evangelicals [Potter].

Two-thirds of the pastors have held teaching positions in schools and colleges, indicating our heart-felt commitment to understanding through education.

We are truly a wide and varied groups of people, called to serve God by serving his people!

"To God be the glory, great things He hath done!"

www.ingramcontent.com/pod-product-compliance
Lightning Source LLC
Chambersburg PA
CBHW070833100426
42813CB00003B/597